How to use this booklet

This booklet aims to help the reader plan a walking tour around Historic Leith. It does not lay down a set walking route and it is left to the reader to select items of interest and devise their

own route using the map provided. Some people may want to devise several separate walks using this material.

The sites mentioned have been numbered, starting with the statue of **Queen Victoria** at the foot of Leith Walk. This was chosen not because it is of any special importance in the history of Leith but rather because it is easy for the visitor to find. Most visitors will approach Leith via Leith Walk and there are numerous bus services that will take you to the Foot of Leith Walk. From this point you have a choice of directions in which to go. You can

go straight through the shopping centre and you will quickly come to **South Leith Parish Church** and **Trinity House** - Sites 2 and 3 in the booklet. Alternatively

you can turn along Duke Street to see **Queen Margaret University College**, **Leith Links** and the Edinburgh **Hindu Mandir** (Sites 4,5 and 6).

Whatever you do and wherever you start from, Leith Local History Society hopes that you will find something to interest you.

Sometimes we mention in the booklet something about the interior of the building concerned. This does not imply that it is open to the public and that you will be able to see the interior.

The following buildings are regularly open to the public:
- **Trinity House** - see item 3 for details
- **Places of religion** are open at times of worship and otherwise by arrangement.
- **Leith Library** - open 10am to 8pm Monday - Thursday, 10am to 5pm on Friday and 9am to 1pm on Saturday.
- **Ocean Terminal** - open during business hours

Other buildings may be open to the public on special occasions - for instance the annual Doors Open Day which usually takes place in September.

1651	The Mercurius Scoticus, one of the first Scottish newspapers, is printed in Leith.
1670	Sir James Stansfield set up a brewery in Leith – probably the largest industrial unit in Scotland at that time.
1680	The teaching of mathematics in Scottish schools is pioneered at Trinity House.
1720	The first dry dock was built in Leith.
1744	The world's first rules of golf are written for a tournament played on Leith Links.
1821	The first steamship service from Leith to London is started.
1832	The first intravenous treatment for cholera is given by Leith physician Dr Thomas Latta.
1838	The Leith-built steamship, *Sirius*, is the first to cross the Atlantic under its own steam.
1838	Leith gets its first railway – a branch of the horse-drawn Edinburgh and Dalkeith Railway.
1841	Charles Drummond manufactures the world's first greetings cards in Leith, bearing the message "*A guid New Year and mony o' them*".
1887	Leith Hospital is the first hospital in Scotland to admit women medical students to its wards for clinical training.
1903	The first purpose-built nautical college in Scotland opens in Leith.
1905	Leith gets electric tramcars – 17 years before Edinburgh.
1910	The first aeroplane to be built and to fly in Scotland is made by Gibsons in Manderson Street, Leith.

"As the Romans crossed the river on their way to Cramond", said James Scott Marshall writing in 1986, "they may have known Inverleith as a settlement near the mouth of the Water of Leith". The earliest cottages in "what came to be known as Leith were built where the river met the Forth estuary. ....Huddled together without any street or thoroughfare" they "occupied that area later bounded by the Shore, the Tolbooth Wynd, Water Street and the Broad Wynd", the Shore developing "where the first inhabitants shored up the river bank to provide anchorage for their boats." Later the name Inverleith was used only for the landward area. Documentary records, wrote John Russell in 1922, began in 1143 and were written by monks, but such information as they gave was "scanty in the extreme".

The Firth of Forth provided abundant fish for the earliest inhabitants who developed the fishing village around the river mouth. But Leith had also other means of winning a livelihood for its rising population who began to sow crops and to keep sheep, cows and poultry in what became, away from the sea, a farming hinterland.

During the Middle Ages trade guilds, known as incorporations in Scotland, were established in Leith in spite of the refusal by Edinburgh to accept their legitimacy. Occupations now being followed included, among others, those of masons, fleshers and coopers and, the largest and wealthiest, the Fraternity of Mariners. St Mary's Church (afterwards South Leith Parish

Church) was erected about 1483 and dedicated to the Blessed Virgin, the patron saint of seamen. The Masters and Mariners headquarters were in Fraternity (later Trinity) House, built in 1555 in the Kirkgate opposite the church. By the 18th century what might be called light industries had proliferated into such areas as glassmaking (producing mainly bottles), sugar refining and the manufacture of soap.

From these early and hard-working times, the development of Leith into the major port of Scotland until it was overtaken by the larger trading and shipbuilding facilities of the Clyde, is a long and fascinating story. It led eventually to the derelict warehouses and gap sites of its mid-20th century decline, then onwards to a splendid revival with, at the present day, new life and vigour returning to the ancient port with its new buildings and businesses, the restoration of its surviving architectural heritage and the creation of a harbour and terminal for cruise liners which is putting Leith on the tourist map as a desirable destination well into the future.

Today the Romans would not recognise the tiny settlement at the river mouth. During the centuries that followed, however, Leith has won, through much toil and many tribulations, the honoured place it now holds in the history of Scotland.

1 Queen Victoria's Statue
Foot of Leith Walk

The statue of Queen Victoria was erected in 1907.
It was unveiled with great pomp and ceremony. In
1913 two side panels were added to commemorate
Queen Victoria's visit to Leith in 1842 and her
review of volunteers who were to serve in the
Boer War.

Queen Victoria did not actually
land in Leith. She arrived by
a steamship that needed the
deep-water facilities at
Granton. She was, however,
greeted by the Provost of Leith
who learnt that she would be
passing through Leith the next
day on her way from Lord
Rosebery's house at Dalmeny
to Dalkeith Palace, the home
of the Duke of Buccleuch. A
triumphal arch was quickly
constructed on Great Junction
Street outside Dr Bell's School
in time for the Queen's arrival.

This is a focal point for the exploration of historic
Leith. From this point you can access either
Great Junction Street, Duke Street, Kirkgate or
Constitution Street, all of which contain buildings
mentioned in this guide.

South Leith Parish Church
Kirkgate

The church was built in 1483 by the trade
incorporations (guilds) of Leith. It was dedicated
to St Mary, patron saint of sailors. King James III
gave 18 shillings to the "*new Kyrk to our Ladie*".

It suffered from looting during the English
invasion in 1544 - known as the "*Rough Wooing*".
In 1560 during the Siege of Leith English artillery
brought down the chancel, transepts and central
tower. Later that year
the Reformation took
place and the
remaining nave was
considered sufficient
for Protestant worship.
So the ruined parts
were not rebuilt. The
church that you see
today was extensively
rebuilt in 1846-47.

 In the porch are the
arms of Mary of Guise and the Royal Arms of
Scotland with the initials of her daughter Mary,
Queen of Scots. Inside there is a magnificent
hammer beam roof, modelled on that of St Isaac's
Church in St Petersburg.

3 Trinity House
Kirkgate

Trinity House was founded as a charity in the 14th century by the mariners of Leith. The Fraternity of Shipowners and Shipmasters collected a tax called Prime Gilt from the ships in the port to fund their charitable work. The present building, designed by Thomas Brown, was built in 1816. It lies on the site of the mariner's medieval hospice, from which the vaults remain, along with two stone plaques that are still visible on the outside wall.

Trinity House played a considerable role in the development, and history, of Leith. In the Firth of Forth, the mariners at one time had the power to license pilots and improve the lights.

Trinity House is now in the care of Historic Scotland. It holds an outstanding collection of maritime artefacts and paintings, some commissioned for the medieval building. Guided tours are available. For more information, please telephone 0131 554 3289.

4 Queen Margaret University College

(Formerly Leith Academy), Duke Street

This impressive building was erected in 1931 for what was then Leith Academy Secondary School. The school has a long history going back to at least 1521. It is not known where the school was based in the early days but from at least 1636 to 1710 it was based in Trinity House. It then moved to the King James Hospital which stood in South Leith Churchyard.

In 1806, a new school was built on Leith Links and it became known as Leith High School. (A later building, dating from 1896 on the same site, still exists as Leith Primary School.) It changed its name to Leith Academy in 1888.

The Leith Links building eventually became too small and the school moved to the Duke Street building in 1931. In 1991 Leith Academy moved to its present site in Academy Park.

The Duke Street building is now the Leith Campus of Queen Margaret University College. About 700 of its students are based there.

5 Golf on Leith Links

The earliest mention of golf in Scotland dates from 1457 when King James II instructed that the game be "*utterly cryt downe and nocht usyt*" as it interfered with lawful, patriotic and essential archery practice. This indicates that golf was already well established. By 1505, however, James IV was

enthusiastically playing the game, as there is a mention of money for the king's golf balls and clubs to "*play at gowf at Leithe*". There were many hazards as the common ground was used for drilling soldiers, exercising horses, drying clothes, grazing cattle, weapons training, holding fairs and breeding food rabbits - not all usually simultaneously!

The world's first rules of golf were drawn up in 1744 to be used on Leith Links and mention the hazards of the soldiers' lines.

> *Rule number 13: Neither trench, Ditch or Dyke, made for the preservation of the Links, nor the scholar's Holes or the Soldier's Lines, shall be accounted a hazard, but the Ball is to be taken out, Tee'd and play'd with any Iron Club.*

A commemorative cairn bears a small plaque which shows the layout of the five original holes.

6 Edinburgh Hindu Mandir
Formerly St Andrews Place Church

The story of this building is one of adaptation to changing circumstances.

It was formerly St Andrews Place Church. People often ask, "*why were there so many churches in Leith?*". Partly the answer lies in the tendency of Presbyterian churches in the past to split over points that were usually concerned with administration rather than doctrine.

The St Andrews Place Church belonged to a group that originally left the Church of Scotland in 1733 over the question of patronage - the right of a

patron (usually a local landowner) rather than the congregation to select a minister.

Eventually patronage was abolished and gradually the wounds were healed with most of the churches coming together again in 1929.

With the changes in population density in Leith and changing patterns of church attendance, this church became surplus to the requirements of the Church of Scotland. The building has now found a new role as a temple, community and cultural centre for the Hindu community of Edinburgh and the Lothians.

Leith Police Station
Formerly Town Hall and Courthouse -
Constitution Street / Queen Charlotte Street

In 1833 Leith became a separate burgh independent of Edinburgh. It retained this status until 1920.

The new burgh had 16 councillors. The Provost also had the honorary title of Admiral. It took over as a base for its operations the building that had already been built in 1827/28 as a Court House. In 1868 the adjoining house at 31 Queen Charlotte Street was reconstructed as an annexe.

Nowadays the entire building is occupied by the Police Station. Inside, the original council chamber survives as it was when the last council meeting took place in 1920.

On the outside of the building there is a plaque commemorating a plebiscite held in January 1920. This was organised to find out the views of Leith people about Edinburgh's proposal to absorb the burgh. The result was 5357 for amalgamation and

29,891 against. Alas it was to no avail and the amalgamation went through.

8 St Mary Star of the Sea

Roman Catholic Church - Constitution Street

Until 1854, Roman Catholics in Leith worshipped
in the Assembly Rooms. It became evident
that there was a need for a church and from
1847 the priest of the area travelled the country
raising money.

Work stated on the new church in 1852. Drawings
by Augustus Pugin were approved and carried out

by his son Edward.
Archbishop Gillies
presided at the first
Eucharist in this new
mission church in
1854. The emphasis
from the first was on
providing a good
education for the
Catholic children
of the area.

By 1900 the church had become too small. A new
aisle was added in 1901 and in 1912 the church
was extensively re-orientated and an apse added.

One of the Church's patrons, J A Hansom (of cab
fame) encouraged Francis Barnett to design the
stained glass for the great west window and two
chancel windows. Michael Donnelly described
them as having *"remarkably rich, sombre and unusual
colour schemes and figure work"*.

9 Assembly Rooms and Exchange Buildings

Constitution Street

The Assembly Rooms, facing Assembly Street, were opened in 1783. At that time most Scottish towns would have had similar buildings which served as a centre for holding balls and other social activities for the wealthier people in the town. Leith was obviously an affluent community to be able to support this type of activity despite its proximity to Edinburgh.

In 1809 Exchange Buildings were added - facing on to the then recently constructed Constitution Street. The Exchange was then the commercial heart of the port of Leith. An account written in 1845 describes the Exchange as containing "*a spacious reading room for the accommodation of mercantile men, a hotel, assembly rooms, sale rooms and library*". This building also contained an impressive ballroom rising through two storeys.

10 Corn Exchange
Constitution Street

On the corner of Constitution Street and Baltic Street stands the Corn Exchange. Leith was a centre of the grain trade in Scotland and much business was undertaken there.

The building was completed in 1862 and cost £6,500. One point to note is the fine sculpted frieze by John Rhind that runs almost the entire length of the building. It depicts cherubs engaged in various commercial and agricultural activities.

While the building was primarily intended for commercial usage, it also provided a meeting place for social gatherings. For instance, on 21st March 1871, a soiree and concert were held there to celebrate the marriage of Queen Victoria's daughter Princess Louise and the Marquis of Lorne. In honour of that event the Town Hall and the Exchange were illuminated that evening.

11 Robert Burns' Statue
Bernard Street

The Leith Burns Appreciation Society erected the statue of Robert Burns in Bernard Street in 1898.

Did Burns have any connection with Leith? When he first came to Edinburgh in November 1786 he had with him a sailing ticket for the *Roselle*. This ship was due to sail from Leith to the West Indies at the end of December 1786. Burns was hoping to get a second edition of his poems published in Edinburgh but if this did not come off he could fall back on an earlier plan to emigrate to Jamaica. As things turned out he did not need to use his ticket - Burns got a new edition of his poems published.

Burns certainly visited Leith. In a letter to his friend Gavin Hamilton he describes having dined at a friend's house in Leith where they "*danced, drank and sang until late enough*" and where he met a very pretty girl.

12 Leith Bank
Bernard Street

In the early 19th century Leith, like a lot of other Scottish towns, had its own locally owned bank. The Leith Banking Company was set up in 1792 with 18 partners, mostly local merchants.

At first it did well. It had branches at Callander, Dalkeith, Galashiels, Langholm and Carlisle. It also had a tent from which it did banking business at agricultural shows and markets.

From 1806 the Bank traded from an elegant two storey building in Bernard Street. It issued its own bank notes. One of its notes depicted King George IV at the King's Landing with the Custom House in the background.

Later it fell on hard times. In 1838 it refused a take-over offered by the Glasgow Union Bank. In 1842 the Leith Banking Company failed.

Lamb's House
Burgess Street

Mary, Queen of Scots, landed at Leith on 19th August 1561 on her return from France. She had not been expected until later that month and no preparations had been made for her reception. She and her retinue were taken to dine in *"Andro Lambis House"* and were escorted to Holyrood later that day.

The present house is not the one that Mary visited. It is, however, a very fine example of an early 17th century Scots merchant's house.

In 1938 it was bought by the 4th Marquis of Bute who presented it to the National Trust for Scotland. In 1961 it was converted into a day centre for the elderly.

The Vaults

Giles Street

From the Middle Ages onwards, Leith was a centre of the wine trade in Scotland. Leith ships sailed to Bordeaux and returned with large quantities of wine for the Court, the Nobility and indeed anyone else who could afford to buy it. Later on there was an extensive trade in wines from Spain and Portugal.

In theory all the wine should have been taken up to Edinburgh for sale. This was difficult as it involved a journey of about a mile and a half over muddy, uneven tracks. Leith merchants found ways around this requirement and the building known as The Vaults has deep cellars or vaults which are believed to have been used for storage of wine since the 15th century.

The building itself dates from 1682 with a fourth storey added in 1785. Nowadays it contains a restaurant and the headquarters of The Scotch Malt Whisky Society.

15 The King's Wark

The Shore

In the Middle Ages many of the cargoes landed at Leith would be for consumption by the royal household. King James I set up the King's Wark - a combined storehouse and arsenal. Over the years the Stewart monarchs extended it so that it also included a royal residence, a naval yard and workshops. There is no evidence that any of the kings actually lived there but they may have used it for short stays when they came to inspect their ships or artillery. Later there was a Custom House there.

Like much else in Leith it was badly damaged in Hertford's raid in 1544. It was rebuilt in the 1560s. In 1575 it was used for the reception of people recovering from the plague. In the 1690s it was destroyed by fire. The present building dates from the early 18th century. The building was restored in the 1970s.

16 The Custom House
Commercial Street

Leith as a major port had a Custom House from a very early date. In the Middle Ages customs duties were either "*petty customs*" or "*great customs*".

Petty customs went into the Common Good Funds of the burgh - in Leith's case they fell into the coffers of Edinburgh. Great customs provided a major source of revenue for the King. Officials

called "*customars*" were appointed to collect the King's customs and ensure that he was not defrauded. At one time the Custom House was located in the King's Wark.

A new Custom House was erected on the northern shore of the river in 1812. It was designed by Robert Reid who was one of the architects involved with the second New Town of Edinburgh.

The building is now used by the National Museums of Scotland for storage. Many people in Leith hope that one day it will become the Museum of Leith.

17 The King's Landing
The Shore

A cast iron tablet marks the spot where King George IV landed on his visit to Scotland on 15th August 1822. He was the first British monarch to visit Scotland since Charles II in 1650.

The visit was stage-managed by Sir Walter Scott. The King landed wearing the uniform of an Admiral - not the flesh-coloured tights and kilt that he later wore at Holyrood Palace.

The visit was a colourful occasion. Glengarry Highlanders and members of the Royal Company of Archers guarded the royal carriage. The Trades Incorporations of Leith were assembled along Bernard Street and Constitution Street, bearing their banners. Each individual had a white rod and was dressed in a blue coat, white vest and trousers with a St Andrews Cross on his hat.

On the North Leith side of the river the Magistrates and Trades of Canongate were similarly assembled.

18 The Ship Inn
The Shore

In April 1779 a mutiny took place outside the Ship Inn. Fifty Highlanders who had been recruited for service in Highland Regiments were ordered to embark on a ship. They thought that they were going to be made to join a Lowland regiment and they refused to go on board.

Two hundred troops from Edinburgh Castle were marched to Leith with orders to take the mutineers prisoner. The major in charge of these troops harangued the Highlanders in English. This achieved nothing, as they did not understand him. A Gaelic speaking sergeant from the castle learnt that the mutineers would open fire if the major did not withdraw his troops.

Eventually they did open fire, killing one of the officers. The troops from Edinburgh Castle then fired on the mutineers, killing twelve of them and wounding twenty. It was probably all a sad misunderstanding compounded by language difficulties.

The Signal Tower
The Shore

This is one of the oldest buildings in Leith. It was built in 1685-86 by Robert Mylne and was originally a windmill. It is said to have been used for milling rape-seed oil. This commodity was probably shipped in from the Baltic ports rather than grown locally. The windmill's site would be ideal for making a quick and easy transfer from incoming ships and certainly there would usually be no shortage of wind to drive it.

In 1805 its domed roof and sails were removed and it was topped with battlements. It was then used as a signal tower from which flag signals could be displayed to let ships making their way into the harbour know the depth of water at the harbour bar.

Along the Shore you will see entrances to Timber Bush and you may wonder about this curious name. Bush is a corruption of *"bourse"* - an exchange or market. So the name means *"timber market"* and reminds us of Leith's long involvement with the timber trade.

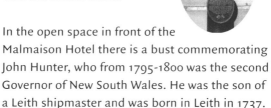

In the open space in front of the Malmaison Hotel there is a bust commemorating John Hunter, who from 1795-1800 was the second Governor of New South Wales. He was the son of a Leith shipmaster and was born in Leith in 1737.

Nearby is an unusual piece of sculpture. It is a statue of Sandy Robertson, a local wine merchant, seated on a bench. There's room to join him on the bench if you wish!

Looking across the river you will see many blocks of modern flats - part of the regeneration of Leith as a desirable housing area. In the 19th century shipyards occupied that area. From one of these came the steamship *Sirius*, the first steamship to cross the Atlantic.

21 The Malmaison Hotel
Formerly the Sailors' Home

This building was built in the Scottish Baronial style and opened in 1885 as the Sailors' Home. It replaced an earlier Sailors' Home in Dock Street.

It had accommodation for 56 seamen and 9 officers. If necessary 50 shipwrecked sailors could be accommodated in dormitories in the attics. The facilities included a dining room, recreation room, reading room, officers' sitting room, bathrooms and lavatories. Altogether a very civilised provision for its time for seafarers who might otherwise have had nowhere to go between ships. It was also used to gather together crews of whaling ships the night before sailing to South Georgia.

Now, as the Malmaison Hotel, it caters for a different category of clientele and provides more luxurious standards of accommodation.

The Harpoon
The Shore

The harpoon preserved on The Shore reminds us of an industry that was once very important in Leith. Nowadays we tend to regard whaling with distaste. In its day it was, however, regarded as a valuable source of food oils and raw materials for industry.

Whaling started in Leith in 1616 and flourished in the 18th century. The whalers sailed to Arctic waters - mainly around Greenland. This type of whaling stopped in 1842.

In 1908 Christian Salvesen & Son sent a whaling fleet from Leith. Now the destination was the Antarctic. A whaling station called *Leith Harbour* was established in South Georgia. By 1911 their whaling fleet was the largest in the world. For many years the whaling industry was a valuable source of employment for Leith people. Whaling ceased in 1963.

The Victoria Swing Bridge
The Shore

Bridges have always been important as a means of connecting North and South Leith. The first bridge was a stone bridge built by the Abbot of Holyrood in 1483. Fixed bridges impeded shipping on the river and that bridge was demolished in the 18th century and replaced by drawbridges that could be lifted to allow shipping to pass.

A swing bridge is another means of allowing shipping to pass. The Victoria Swing Bridge was completed in 1874. It carried double rail and road tracks with a footpath along each side. When it was built it was the largest swing bridge in the United Kingdom. Nowadays the rail tracks have been removed and with a new road bridge running parallel to it, it is solely for pedestrian use.

For those interested in the technical aspects it was originally hydraulically operated but was later replaced with a bowstring swing bridge.

The Scottish Executive
Victoria Quay

This prize-winning building was started in 1993, as part of the redevelopment of Victoria Quay. The project involved building two new bridges and diverting the main access road.

It was released to the then Scottish Office in 1995 and allowed the accommodation of more departments in one place than ever before. In 1999, following the election of the Scottish Parliament, it passed to the Scottish Executive.

Particular care was given to artistic features in the interior. Paintings were borrowed from the Scottish Arts Council's collection and permanent features were also created.

In addition to the Scottish Executive building, housing and retail development of the quay has also taken place. An attractive gateway commemorating the quay's fishing past completes the area.

25 The Citadel
Dock Street

In the 1650s Leith was garrisoned by a Cromwellian army under General Monck. He was concerned about the defences of Leith and decided to build a Citadel in North Leith. Edinburgh Town Council contributed £5,000 towards the total cost of £100,000.

Work began in 1653 and it was near completion by 1654. John Ray, an English naturalist, described it as "*one of the best fortifications that we ever beheld, passing fair and sumptuous*".

After the Restoration it was briefly used for industrial purposes and also became a fashionable place to live. One of the first genuinely Scottish newspapers, the Mercurius Caledonius, started here in 1660.

Edinburgh lobbied for it to be demolished. It had a brief moment of military activity in 1715 when some Jacobite supporters occupied it for a few days. Gradually, however, it was demolished and all that remains today is one stone arch.

26 St Ninian's Chapel
Quayside Street

This is the oldest surviving building in Leith. Robert Ballantyne, Abbot of Holyrood, built it in 1493.

The chapel was probably in ruins after English raids in 1544 and 1547. After the Reformation the people of North Leith rebuilt it. In 1606 the parish of North Leith was created and the old chapel became its parish church.

The church was rebuilt and extended in the late 17th century. This was when the distinctive Dutch style steeple was built. It bears the date 1675.

Eventually it became too small for the congregation. A new church was built in Madeira Street and opened in 1816. The old church was sold and used for commercial purposes. In 1997 the buildings were purchased by the Cockburn Conservation Trust and restored for use as offices.

27 Guru Nanak Gurdwara (Sikh Temple)

Sheriff Brae

The Sikh Temple for Edinburgh, the Lothians and Fife is situated at the top of Sheriff Brae. The orange flag of the Gurdwara has flown since 30 June 1976. Around 400 worship there, more on festive occasions. Their bleakest moment was in 1989 when the building was a target of arson. Recovery was swift and the temple was reinaugurated by Lord Provost Eleanor McLaughlin at a huge multi-faith gathering. Since then the community has continued to grow and there are now plans to alter the interior to allow for more room.

The building started life as St Thomas's Church. It was built in 1843 as a memorial to the Gladstone family by Sir John Gladstone of Fasque, father of the Victorian politician. John Henderson was the architect not only of the church but also the manse and nearby school and almshouses. A Zeppelin raid destroyed the manse in April 1916 but miraculously the church was undamaged. Union with Junction Road Church took place in May 1975.

28 Victoria Baths
Junction Place

Known to generations of Leithers as *"Vickies"*, the history of the Victoria Baths can be seen on the building itself. It was opened on 30th June 1899 by Provost Richard Mackie and was a proud achievement for Leith Town Council.

The Council appointed a Baths Sub-Committee that met at least seven times to decide on such matters as appointment of a heating engineer

and attendants, the organisation of the opening and making sure that the costs were reasonable.

Leith Swimming Club used the swimming pool from the start and held regular galas.

At a time when few private houses had bathrooms, the Victoria also provided private plunge baths at either 6d for first class or 3d for second class. Season tickets were available for both swimming and bathing.

After some deliberation the Baths subcommittee agreed to open the baths on Sunday mornings between 7am and 8.30am. For these late Victorians cleanliness was close to godliness!

Dr Bell's School
Great Junction Street

Dr Andrew Bell was born in St Andrews in 1753. He studied at St Andrews University and was ordained into the Church of England. He served at an Episcopal Chapel in Leith and then became an army chaplain in India.

He was appointed as superintendent of the Madras Male Orphanage Asylum - an orphanage for soldiers' sons. There he devised a system under which some of the brighter boys were given a lesson and then had to teach the other boys. He brought this system, known as the "*Madras System*" back to Britain and by the time of his death in 1832 there were about 12,000 schools using it.

Dr Bell left £10,000 to found a school in Leith to be operated on his system. The building known as Dr Bell's School was opened in 1839. It was later taken over by Leith School Board and the Madras system was no longer used.

There was a particularly strong interest to decorate Leith in the early 1980s as gable ends of buildings became exposed and new precincts were developed.

The most striking gable end mural is in North Junction Street. Measuring about 100 square feet it was painted by Paul Grime and Tim Chalk. School pupils and pensioners supplied the subjects on which the mural is based. Shipbuilding, dock life, children at play, a Gaiety Theatre programme and a strike demonstration can all be seen. Other gable end murals can be seen in Admiralty Street and Bonnington Road.

Three large hangings in the library are reminders of the *Pictures of Leith* project and are a wonderful representation of Leith history and community pride. The pop art figures by the Citadel Youth Club capture the spirit of their age. Smaller items such as cast concrete "*wheatsheaf*" bollards are in the Swanfield industrial area.

It is good to note that function and design can combine to produce interest and a smile.

31 Norwegian Church
North Junction Street

In 1863 a divinity graduate called Johan Cordt Harmens Storjohn from Bergen in Norway came to Edinburgh to study. He found that Scandinavian seamen had no church in which to worship and committed himself to establishing one.

In 1865 the first pastor arrived and in 1869 the church was built. It was designed by a local architect who adapted a Danish design.

By the church door there is a boulder bearing an inscription in Norwegian. The story is that this boulder was brought to Leith in a ship, which ran aground. When it was refloated and docked, the bolder was found in the bow section and was given a final resting place by the church door.

For many years the Church continued with its mission of attending to the pastoral needs of seamen. It has now become the home of the Leith School of Art.

32 Ocean Terminal and Leith Docks

The Royal Yacht Britannia is berthed to the west of the Ocean Terminal Shopping and Leisure Complex, which was built on the site of the famous Ramage and Ferguson, and later Henry Robb, shipyards. Many thousands of ships were built by the hundreds of thousands of men who were employed in the yards.

The Kobenhaven, which was built by Ramage and Ferguson, was the largest sailing ship ever built

in the UK; launched in 1921, she was lost at sea in 1929.

In previous centuries Leith was Scotland's number one port. There was constant commercial traffic with coal exported and grain, wine, timber and other commodities imported.

During the early 1900s steamships constantly sailed in and out of Leith Docks. There were daily sailings to Queensferry, Aberdour, Kirkcaldy, North Berwick, and cruises round the Bass Rock, as well as sailings to London three days a week and, for the rich, cruises to Holland and Belgium.

Nowadays, Leith is still a busy commercial port as well as a popular destination for cruise ships from all over the world.

33 North Leith Parish Church
Madeira Street

Opened in 1816, the present North Leith Parish Church was intended to be the centre-piece of Leith New Town. William Burn designed it along very similar lines to Falkirk Town Hall.

It was built to generous specifications and with the best of materials. Single lengths of pitch pine from America, carried over the Atlantic in the keels of ships as ballast, remain intact as 70-foot joists across the building. The ashlar stone came from Craigleith.

The design depends on symmetry. It is shaped as a true Presbyterian church, with the pulpit central and prominent so that the Word of the Lord may be heard by all. With its plastered walls, light colours, unadorned walls and clear upper storey windows that catch the sun throughout the day, the church which has remained basically unaltered for almost 200 years is the finest building in the neighbourhood.

34 Leith Fort
North Fort Street

On 14th September 1779 John Paul Jones, the American pirate (or naval hero if you are American) sailed into the Firth of Forth with his squadron of ships. He hoped to raise £200,000 as a ransom for Leith and if this was not forthcoming he intended to reduce it to ashes.

On Sunday, 17th September crowds gathered on the Fife coast and on the shore and pier of Leith watching the enemy ships. In Leith one of the ministers prayed fervently and his prayers were apparently answered. When the ships were abreast of Inchkeith a violent gale blew up making it impossible to land.

The Fort was then built to provide some defence against attacks from the sea. It was garrisoned by the Royal Artillery but never fired a shot in anger. It was demolished in the 1950s and only the outer walls and a gatehouse remain.

Thomas Morton Hall
Ferry Road

This building is part of a complex formerly known as *Leith Town Hall*. It was never a town hall in the sense of being the headquarters of a town council as it was part of a complex of public buildings put up after the amalgamation of Leith with Edinburgh. Nowadays it is the scene of many local activities and has a marriage suite upstairs.

Thomas Morton was a local shipbuilder whose shipyard was, in the early 19th century, on a site

by Junction Bridge not far from where the Hall now stands. He invented a widely used device for hauling ships out of the water for cleaning and repair without having to use a dry dock. This was known as *Morton's Patent Slip*.

He died in 1832 at the age of 51 and is buried in South Leith Churchyard. The hall was named after him to keep alive the name of a man who made a significant contribution to the standing of Leith.

36 Leith Library
Ferry Road

This bright airy semi-circular building at the corner of Ferry Road and North Junction Street was originally opened in 1929. It suffered extensive bomb damage on the night of 7 April 1941 and was out of commission until 1955.

When it first opened palm trees mirrored the pillars and silence was probably necessary because of the parquet flooring. The layout was different too, as there were a separate reference area and newsroom.

Nowadays there are carpets throughout. The reference library accommodates the Registrar's Office and the newsroom is now a very well used community hall. Silence is rare!

What has not changed is the staff's commitment to answering enquiries and providing the right books (of whatever format) to the public of Leith. If you have any questions about old (or new) Leith, this is the place to ask.

Here is a selection of books used in this booklet.
They will also provide further information on
the topics.

Primary Sources

Leith Burgh Council Minutes 1885-1920
Edinburgh and Leith Post Office Directories,
1845-1974
Memorial Inscriptions of South Leith Churchyard
ed. J.S.Marshall (1963)
Memorial Inscriptions of North Leith Churchyard
ed. J.S.Marshall (1963)

Oral History Sources

Leith Local History Project: *Leith Lives- A Walk in
the Past* (1989)
Fort Community Wing Friday Women's Group:
Die Hards o' Leith (1995)

Books

Dick, Iain: *A Wee Look at Leith* (1984)
Donnelly, Michael: *Scotland's Stained Glass* (1997)
Gifford, McWilliam and Walker: *The Buildings
of Scotland, Edinburgh* (1984)
Hutton, Guthrie: *Old Leith* (1995)
Irons, James C.: *Leith and its Antiquities from
Earliest Time*, 2 vols. (1898)
McDougall, Ian: *Voices of Leith Dockers* (2001)

Marshall, James Scott: *The Church in the Midst -South Leith Parish Church through Five Centuries (1983);*
Life and Times of Leith (1986);
North Leith Parish Church - the First 500 Years (1993)
Mowat, Sue: *The Port of Leith, its History and its People (1994)*
Mullay, Sandy: *The Edinburgh Encyclopaedia (1996)*
Russell, J: *The Story of Leith (1922)*
Wallace, Joyce: *Traditions of Trinity and Leith (1985);*
Further Traditions of Trinity and Leith (1990)

Many of these books are now out of print but may be borrowed from Leith Library or consulted at the Edinburgh Room within Edinburgh Central Library on George IV Bridge. This library also has a wide range of photographs, maps and census details.

The extensive Leith Collection of artefacts, photographs and oral history material is held by The City of Edinburgh Council at The People's Story Museum, Canongate. It is intended that the Collection be permanently displayed in a future Leith Museum.

Notes